AF255778

Set, Hut!

A Manifesto for Common Sense Football

Richie Petersen

M&B Global Solutions Inc.
Green Bay, Wisconsin (USA)

Set, Hut!

A Manifesto for Common Sense Football

ISBN: 978-1-942731-56-6

Published by M&B Global Solutions Inc.
Green Bay, Wisconsin (USA)

Dedication

To the football fans who are as frustrated as I am over the state of coaching throughout the sport. If this book saves one team and its fans from any amount of heartache, it's worth it.

Also dedicated to any coaches who adopt the Madden Scheme.

Set, Hut!!

Contents

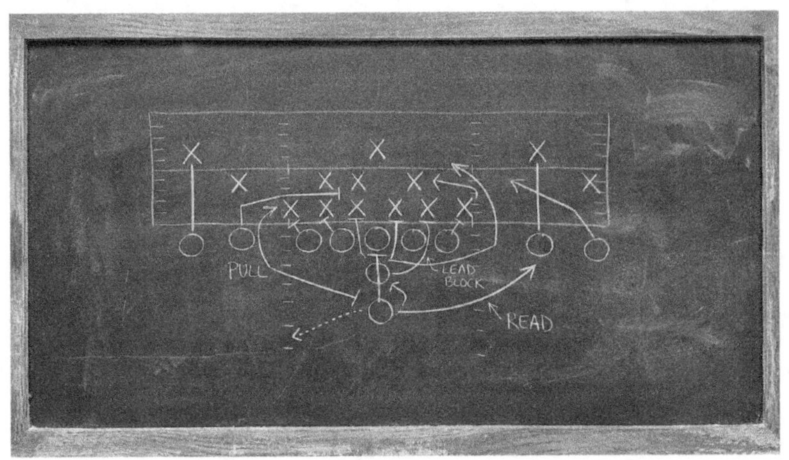

Introduction

Some of this stuff is so basic that I can't believe I even have to say it. But after studying more than 120,000 plays over the last three seasons (2023-2025), I've learned one thing: **Common sense is not that common in the National Football League or Division 1 college football.**

The same mistakes show up every week – clock disasters, short-yardage plays, ego calls, mental errors, bad situational football – and they cost teams games. It shouldn't be this hard. Football rewards clarity, discipline, and simplicity. This report is about getting back to that.

If you want to build a winning program, it starts with the mindset of the people in the building. Before scheme, before talent, before anything else, you need a culture that refuses to beat itself. Everything you do – every meeting, every drill, every standard – either builds and supports that culture or destroys it.

A fast-paced, simple, hard-nosed offensive scheme powers the aggressive mentality that serves as the foundation for this culture. It emphasizes getting on the ball, going quick count, and running the ball down the opponent's throat.

Culture isn't a slogan or a catchphrase or just sometimes. Culture is the operating system. Always.

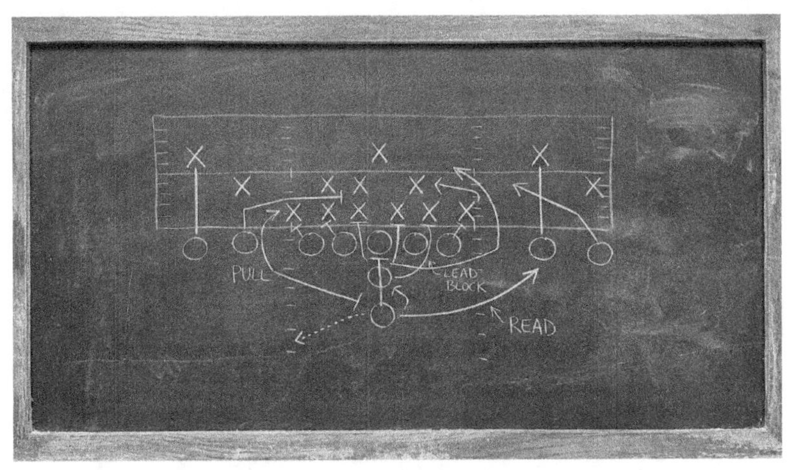

Chapter 1

Culture

You don't need a microscope to see culture. It shows up in results. Look at the difference between the New York Jets and the New England Patriots. One franchise hasn't made the playoffs in fifteen years and counting. The other went to ten Super Bowls in twenty-five years. That's not luck. That's not talent swings. That's culture: standards, accountability, and clarity from top to bottom.

Those aren't the only examples. Look at the consistently good organizations: the Baltimore Ravens, Pittsburgh Steelers, Kansas City Chiefs, Buffalo Bills, Los Angeles Rams. Different coaches, different quarterbacks, different eras, same results. Why? Because they have alignment. They have structure. They have a culture that survives injuries, roster turnover, and bad Sundays.

Now look at the consistently awful teams: the Cleveland Browns, New Orleans Saints, Miami Dolphins, New York Jets, New York Giants. A new head coach every couple of years. No continuity. No identity. No structure. You can't build a winning program when you're rebuilding the foundation every twenty-four months or less. Losing *becomes* the culture.

Your culture is built from the top down. Ownership, the general manager, coaching staff, and players all need to be on the same page. Consistent rules, practices, habits. A way of life around the building. Everyone buying into the same philosophy. Everyone accountable to the person next to them. Playing for each other.

Football is the ultimate team game. Every piece must be in its place to have success. That's why culture is so important. Everything flows from it. Culture is the difference between a team that beats itself and a team that forces everyone else to play perfect football just to keep up. But culture means nothing if the team can't play fast, finish drives, and hold up for four quarters. Standards only matter when they show up in how you play.

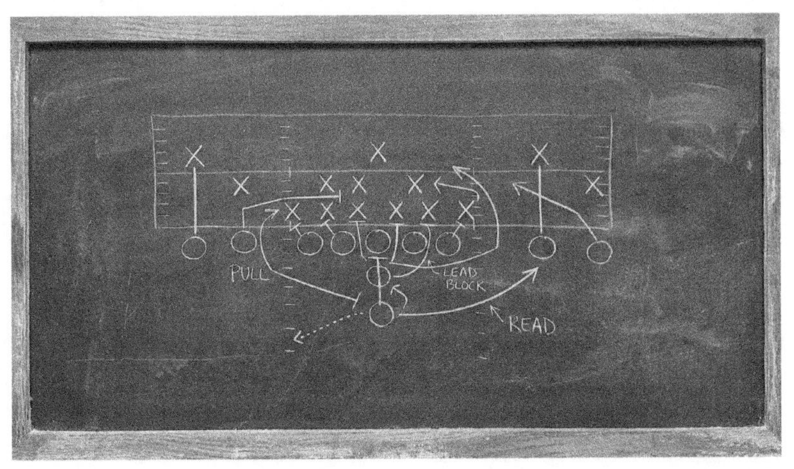

Chapter 2

Conditioning

Conditioning is the first visible expression of your culture. It's the part you can't hide, fake, or talk your way through.

You can talk about toughness and culture all you want, but conditioning is where it shows up. It's the difference between a team that plays fast in September and a team that's still playing fast in December.

You can't shortcut it. Conditioning exposes every lie in your program.

Conditioning is a Year-Round Standard

Conditioning isn't just running gassers in August. It's a year-round commitment. It's weights, sprints, footwork, blocking drills, tackling circuits, change-of-direction work, and position-specific cond itioning. It's the offseason program. It's the way you train in March, April, May, June. The expectation is that players show up to camp already in great shape, not using camp to get in shape.

A well-conditioned team just looks different. They finish blocks. They finished runs. They finish drives. They finish games. They don't tap out in the fourth quarter. They don't need to substitute every two plays. They don't break down when the game gets long and heavy. Conditioning is a foundation for everything else you want to be. But conditioning alone doesn't build a team. It just gives you the raw material. What matters next is how you communicate, teach, and lead.

A team can only play as cleanly and as fast as it is coached. Players reflect the clarity of the message they receive. If the coaching is sloppy, the football will be sloppy. If the coaching is sharp, the football will be sharp. Coaching is the delivery system for everything you believe.

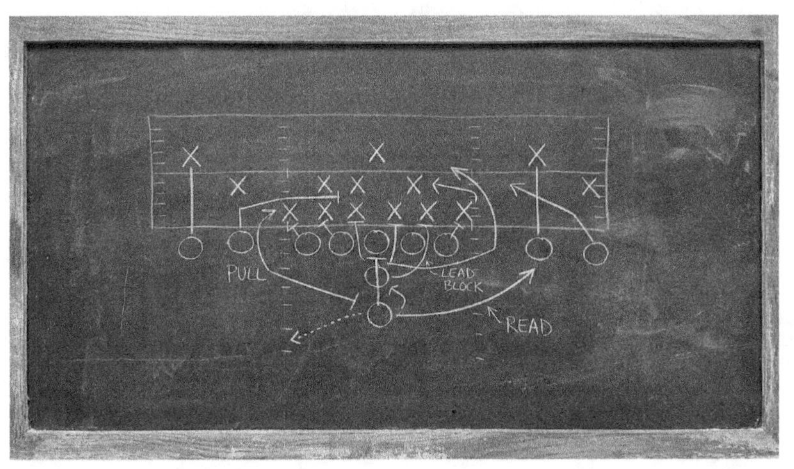

Chapter 3

The Head Coach

Coaching is accountability in real time. It's a daily process of turning expectations into habits and habits into results. A team will only be as disciplined as a coach demands, as detailed as the coach teaches, and as tough as a coach reinforces. You can't hide from the truth on tape, and coaching is the truth-teller.

The best coaches don't confuse players with volume. They teach with clarity. They communicate with purpose. They eliminate gray area. They make the complex simple and the simple automatic. They build rules, not exceptions. They built players who can solve problems on the field without looking to the sideline.

Bad coaching shows up the same way every time: wasted downs, wasted timeouts, wasted opportunities, bad play calls, clock management issues, dumb penalties, and the list goes on.

Good coaching shows up in the details: alignment, leverage, spacing, timing, communication. It shows up in how a team handles third down, the red zone, two-minute and four-minute drills, and backed-up situations. It shows up in how a team responds to adversity.

Coaching isn't all about speeches. It's about standards. It's about teaching the same thing the same way every day until it becomes habit, who you are. It's about eliminating confusion before it becomes a mistake on game day. It's about building a team that knows exactly what it is and how it wins.

The Four Modes of the Head Coach

The head coach operates in distinct modes, each with its own purpose and energy. Players may not always understand him, but they always feel him.

1. Full Team Meetings - The Enigma

In front of the entire team, he's controlled, stern, and almost mysterious. He doesn't waste words. He doesn't perform. He sets the standard with presence alone. Players walk out knowing exactly what's expected, even if they can't fully explain how he made them feel it. This is where the culture is declared. Ideally, he should show up two minutes before the meeting, look at the players, and say, "Men, we know what needs to be done." Then walk out of the room. An enigma. A soul passing in the night.

2. Practice and Position Groups - The Teacher

Up close, he's sharper, more personal, more precise. He'll raise his voice when he needs to, but it's never emotional. It's targeted. He knows which buttons to push, when to challenge, and when to teach. He can be demanding one moment and encouraging the next. Your best friend or your biggest critic? This is where habits are built and details are corrected.

3. Game Day - The Stabilizer

On game day, he becomes something else entirely. Calm. Positive. Unshakable. He doesn't add pressure, he removes it. He reminds players who they are, what they're built of, and why they are ready. He's the steady voice amid the chaos, the emotional anchor the team leans on. His demeanor becomes the team's demeanor, a never-let-them-see-you-sweat presence.

4. Press Conferences - The Shield

He becomes something else entirely with the media. Cold, short, unhelpful. He gives them nothing, no emotion, no entertainment, no headlines. Reporters walk in hoping for clarity and walk out frustrated. That's intentional. He absorbs all the attention so the team doesn't have to. He becomes the story, so the players never are. He takes the heat so the locker room stays cool.

This is the brilliance of coaches like Bill Belichick. He wasn't rude for the sake of being rude, he was strategic. If the media spent the week hating him, debating him, or trying to decode him, they weren't talking about the players. They weren't creating noise inside the building. This was the brilliance of Belichick. A great head coach knows how to weaponize unfriendliness. He becomes a lightning rod so the team can work in anonymity.

Coaching defines who you are. Scheme defines how you win. One is the voice, the other is the blueprint. When the two align, the team plays with purpose and poise. When they don't, everything falls apart. They go hand in hand.

Chapter 4 is about the structure that holds the entire identity together.

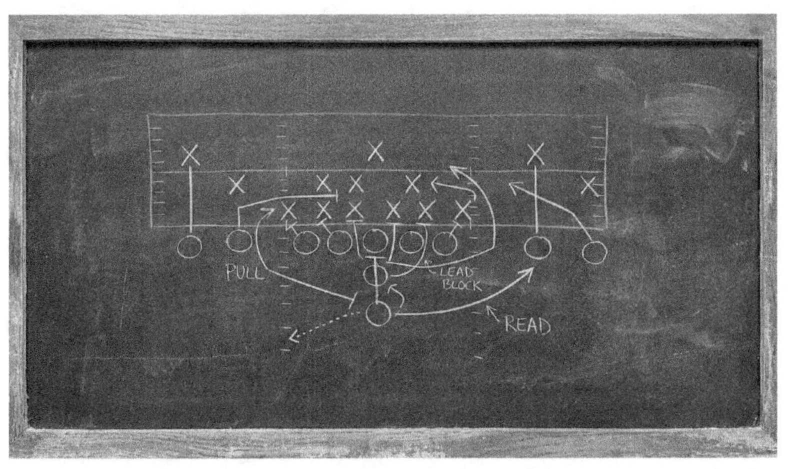

Chapter 4
Scheme

A great scheme is built on clarity. Not volume. Not cleverness. Clarity.

Players don't need a playbook full of exceptions, they need rules they can trust under pressure. The best schemes make the game simple, fast, and honest. Bad schemes try to be everything. They chase trends. Drown players in details. They look good on a whiteboard and fall apart on game day.

A bad scheme forces players to think when they should be reacting. A good scheme fits the players you have. It builds around strengths, hides weaknesses, and evolves without losing its core. It's simple enough to teach and flexible enough to adjust. The truth is simple: *If your scheme is clear, your football will be clear. If your scheme is muddy, your football will be muddy.*

The John Madden Scheme

Every coach eventually has to plant a flag. You can study every system in football, you can borrow ideas from everywhere, but at some point you have to decide what you believe in. What you're willing to hang your name on. What you're willing to run in the biggest moments of your life. For me, that identity is the John Madden Scheme—aka Bowling Ball, Sledgehammer, or Blocking Sled Scheme. Call it what you will, the point is the same. *We play simple, we play downhill, we play with discipline and force.*

This scheme is built on three pillars:

1. Clarity over Complexity

Players don't need a binder. They need rules. They need answers. They need to know exactly what to do when the situation changes. The Madden Scheme allows players to play fast, not think slowly.

2. Violence with Purpose

This isn't finesse football. This is controlled aggression. This is leverage, angles, and body-on-body truth. This is a scheme that demands toughness because it rewards toughness. Simple, but not easy.

3. Tempo as a Weapon

We don't let the defense breathe. We don't let them substitute. We don't let them disguise. We force them to line up, declare themselves, and survive the next snap. Tempo is clarity through controlled chaos. It's on the ball, set-hut. No huddle, no subs.

The Madden Scheme is not cute. It's not trendy. It's not built for clinics or white boards. It's built for game day s. It's built for December. It's built to bully the defense, to humiliate and dominate. It's built for the fourth quarter, when the whole stadium knows what's coming and still can't stop it.

It's a scheme that says:
We're coming right at you.
We're not hiding.
We're not tricking you.
We're unapologetic.

It's honest football.
It's violent football.
It's **winning** football.

In the Madden Scheme, the first two to three drives are smash-mouth, run-dominant football. On the ball, no huddle, no trickery. Up the gut, off tackle, sweeps. The offensive line thrives in this style of play. In a sprinter's stance, no audibles, knowing exactly when the ball will be snapped. They are just like the blocking sled drills that John Madden loved so much.

The D-line will be gassed by the third play, but if the offense doesn't sub, the defense can't. I can see defenders faking injuries just to get a break. I don't know why no one has ever tried this philosophy. It makes perfect sense if you have a below-average quarterback or offensive line. It's much easier to explode off the ball than to pass block, where the first step is retreating while the defense's best athletes come at you full speed. Where's the common sense?

Especially on late-down, short-yardage plays—it should be on the ball, "Set-Hut!" Every second the O-line is in their stance, listening to audibles, legs burning, the advantage goes to the defense. Just snap the damn ball!

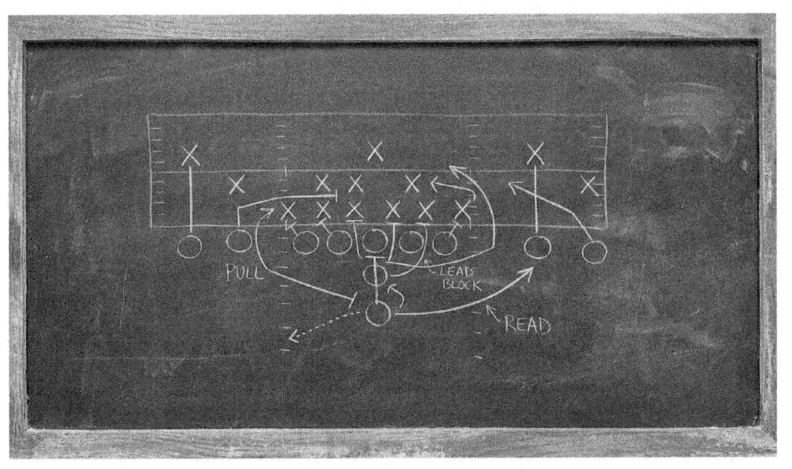

Chapter 5
Situational Football

Situational football is where everything you've built gets tested. Identity, conditioning, coaching and scheme all matter, but they only matter if they show up when the game demands answers. Most teams practice situations. Few master them. Fewer win because of them. Situational football is the hidden curriculum of winning. It's the part of the game that casual fans don't understand and bad teams don't respect.

But the truth is simple: **games are won and lost in situations, not in the middle of the field.** Great teams don't just rise to the moment, they fall back on their situational training.

Third Down – The Money Down

Third down reveals everything about a team. Your identity, your discipline, your ability to execute under pressure, and even your weaknesses. Offensively, third down is about clarity. You have answers versus man, answers versus zone, versus pressure. You don't need 100 plays, you need five to ten that you trust. Defensively, third down is about forcing hesitation, making the QB hold the ball, making the offensive coordinator guess. If you can't win third down, you won't win most games.

Red Zone – Who You Really Are

The field shrinks, the windows tighten, and the margin for error disappears. In the red zone you can't hide, you can't trick people, you can't rely on space. You must run the ball effectively, protect the quarterback, and win one-on-ones. That's it. Red zone football is honesty, toughness and executions. Championship teams finish drives. Average teams kick field goals. Bad teams turn it over. The red zone is one key to victory.

Two-Minute Drill – Controlled Urgency

Two-minute football is clarity under stress. It's comm unication, tempo and trust. Knowing exactly where the ball needs to go and how fast you need to move. Getting out of bounds to stop save a timeout. Getting on the ball quickly. The best two-minute teams don't panic, rush or waste time. They operate with urgency, not chaos. Quarterbacks become leaders and coaches become decisive.

Backed Up – Don't Blink

When you're backed up against your goal line, the whole stadium tightens. Especially on the road, the crowd gets loud, the defense gets greedy, and one mistake could cost you six points. Backed-up football is about poise and integrity. Get a first down. Flip the field. Keep the crowd out of the game. Live to fight the next drive. You don't necessarily need a touchdown, but you definitely need space. Punting isn't always a bad thing.

Goal Line – Will vs. Will

Goal line is the purest form of football. There are no secrets, no disguises, just leverage, pad level and violence. Sure, a Philly Special can work if timed right, but for the most part, the toughest, most disciplined team wins at the goal line. You find out who wants it more, who's willing to sacrifice, who's built for December. Goal line football is truth, and the truth is: get on the ball and slam it down their throat. Set-hut! But don't run into a packed box. Play-action bootleg can be a sure thing against a packed box. Be smart, trust your scheme. Win the play.

Middle Eight – The Hidden Edge

The last four minutes of the first half and first four of the second half decide more games than people realize.
- Steal a possession
- Score before the half
- Score on the first drive of the second half
- Flip momentum
- Control the script

The Middle Eight is where smart, well-coached teams separate. Bill Belichick was a master of getting the double dip. Defering the kickoff to receive in the second half, and scoring late in the first half generates back-to-back possessions. Brilliant!

Momentum – The Invisible Opponent

Some don't believe in momentum. It's not tangible, something you can see. But you can definitely feel it. Momentum is real. You can lose a game in a handful of snaps if you don't manage it. Great teams stop momentum swings before they become avalanches, especially on the road. Scheme and a solid run game are keys to blocking momentum, as is keeping composure when it all seems to be falling around you.

Discipline, control, integrity – these are the keys to keeping momentum on your side. Bad teams let one mistake become three. They let momentum snowball into a crushing force. Championship teams respond immediately. Momentum isn't magic, it's emotional discipline.

Special Teams – The Overlooked Aspect

Many think they know how important special teams are, but it's mostly lip service. In reality, special teams can make or break a game or a season. Bad habits seem to pile up, the same mistakes over and over. This happens when not enough time is dedicated to special teams in practice. Great teams and coaches know this importance, work on it, and take pride in not making mistakes. Have a solid special teams coach, put in the time and effort, and know that it won't cost you games. It just might be a game saver.

Complementary Football – The Whole Picture

Offense, defense and special teams aren't separate units, they're one organism. When one side struggles, the others must compensate. When one side dominates, the others capitalize. It's an equilateral triangle. Pull one side out, the other two collapse upon themselves. Complementary football is maturity, awareness, and understanding the flow of the game. Bad teams play three separate games, great teams play one.

Clock Management and Game Management Assistants – The Missing Coaches

Every NFL team has coordinators, assistants, analysts, and specialists, but almost none have what I feel is truly needed: full-time clock management and game management assistant coaches. These two roles decide games every single week.

Possession math counts. All of it. Timeouts. Replay challenges. End-of-half strategy. End-of-game strategy. Fourth-down decisions. Field position. Risk tolerance. Momentum control. Most teams leave these decisions to the head coach in real time while he's also managing players, emotions, officials, substitutions, injuries, and the entire operation. It's too much. It's unrealistic. It's outdated. Clock management is a job. Game management is a job. They deserve full-time experts.

A Clock Management Coach handles:
- Timeout strategy
- Field position analytics
- Momentum control
- Play clock discipline
- Sideline communication

A Game Management Coach handles:
- Fourth down decisions
- Field position analytics
- Risk vs Reward strategies
- Opponent tendencies
- Critical pass vs run situations

These two coaches work together every day, every week, every game. They are year-round hires, 365 days, studying film and every possible situation that might occur at any point of a game. With a voice in the head coach's ear, they should be as important as the OC and DC. How many games are you yelling at the TV in critical moments, "Call timeout! Stop the clock! Get out of bounds! Kick the field goal!"

The list goes on and on. I believe the teams that hire these two positions, full time, will have a tremendous advantage. (If so, call me up! I'm your man!)

Situational football is where games are won, but it's not where programs are built. Situations expose you. They reveal whether your identity is real or just lip service. If you don't have clarity, discipline and alignment, the moments will find you.

And that brings us to the finish. None of this matters unless you can live it every day. The final chapter isn't about football. It's about the standard that holds everything together.

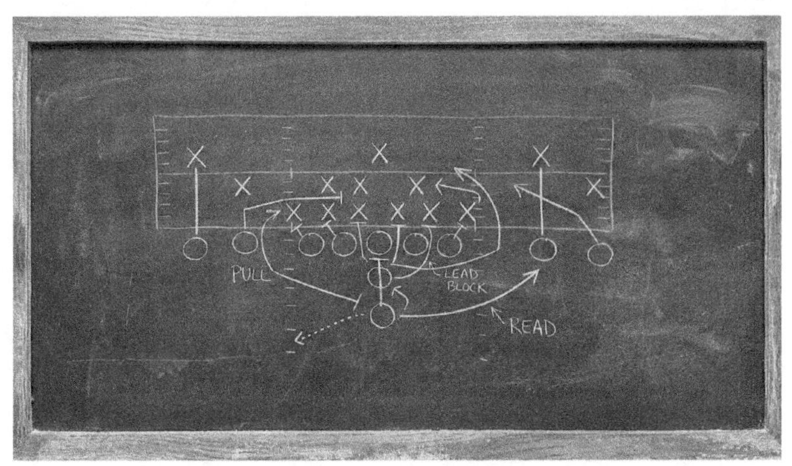

Chapter 6

The Finish

Football is a simple game made complicated by coaches who don't understand what matters. The truth is this: winning is not an accident. It's not luck. It's not talent alone. Winning is the accumulation of small, disciplined decisions made over and over again.

- Identity
- Conditioning
- Coaching
- Scheme
- Situational Football

These aren't just chapters, they're commitments. They're the pillars of a program that knows who it is and refuses to be anything else. The finish is where all of it becomes real.

The Standard

Every program has a standard. Some don't enforce it. Many don't live it. Most don't even know what it is.

The Standard is not a slogan on the wall. It's not a speech. It's not a hashtag.

The Standard is how you show up on a random Tuesday in March. It's how you respond after a loss. It's how you practice when no one is watching. It's how you handle the moments that don't make the highlight reel. The Standard is the finished product.

Consistency over Intensity

Anyone can be intense for a day. Anyone can work hard when they feel good. Anyone can talk culture. But consistency is the separator.

Consistency is boring. It's unglamorous. It's the thing that wins when talent fades and emotions swing. It's absolutely necessary to be successful. The finish is consistency. It's the discipline to do the right thing long after the feeling is gone.

The Program

A great program is not built on plays or players. It's not built on stars or hype. A real program is built on:

- Clarity
- Discipline
- Toughness
- Communication
- Accountability
- The refusal to beat yourself

Every single person in the building being on the same page. You don't need to be perfect, you just need to be aligned. When identity matches conditioning, when coaching matches scheme, when situational football matches preparation, you become very hard to beat. That's the Program.

The Finish Is Every Day

The finish isn't the fourth quarter. It's not the last drive or the final rep. The finish is every day you decide to live by your standard. Every day you choose clarity over chaos. Discipline over emotion. Every day you choose to put in the work. The finish is not an event. It's a lifestyle.

The Last Word

Football is a game of inches, but programs are built in miles. Miles of habits. Miles of decisions. Miles of discipline.

You don't rise to the level of your goals—you fall to the level of your standards. Standards are non-negotiable and absolute. If you build the right standards, if you live them, enforce them and finish them, you give yourself a chance to win every time you set foot on the field.

That's the truth.
That's the program.
That's the FINISH.

About the Author

Richie Petersen is an avid and knowledgeable sports fan who grew up in Tillamook, Oregon, playing whatever sport was in season, year round. It was a different time with no social media, no video games, and no computers. His passion for football evolved through the years and eventually became his favorite sport.

This book comes as a result of watching too much horrendous coaching and play calling over the past decades. Richie earned a bachelor of science degree in communications from Oregon State University, where he had a tryout with the basketball team, and remains a diehard fan of the Beavers today from his adopted home of Kaua'i, Hawai'i.